MW01488722

Welcome to YOUR PLACE CALLED "there"

Andrew Wommack

Published by Andrew Wommack Ministries, Inc.
Woodland Park, CO 80863

ISBN 13 TP: 978-1-59548-734-6

For Worldwide Distribution, Printed in the USA

1 2 3 4 5 6 / 28 27 26 25

Contents

Would you like to get more out of this teaching?

Scan the QR code to access this teaching in video or audio formats to help you dive even deeper as you study.

Accessing the teaching this way will help you get even more out of this booklet.

Introduction

Have you ever wanted to serve God but don't know where to start? Do you dream about going into ministry, starting a business, or even going back to school, but don't feel comfortable leaving behind the security of your career? Do you spend time weighing the pros and cons of stepping into what the Lord has called you to do with your life?

I've met many people over the years who believe they've been called to attend Charis Bible College, but they're hesitant to commit to it. For a lot of those people, it may mean relocating across the country, quitting their jobs, or moving away from family and friends.

Maybe you have an idea of what God has planned for your life, but you are concerned about how things are going to happen or how bills are going to be paid. I've met a lot of people who are waiting for just the right circumstances to start serving God. They tell me that they need to sell their house first, or that they have a few more years until they receive their full retirement benefits.

When people say these things, I typically respond by saying, "Well, I guess God didn't realize that when He called you." That usually catches them off guard. But then I remind them that, in fact, God did know those things and He is going to provide something even better if they are willing to follow Him.

Just past the main gate of our Charis campus in Woodland Park, Colorado, is a big green and yellow sign that reads, "Welcome to your place called 'there.'" We put up that sign to remind our students of the story of the Prophet Elijah, who was called to certain places where the Lord would provide for him (1 Kgs. 17).

Elijah would have had plenty of good reasons not to do what God called him to do, beginning with the threat of losing his life. But Elijah trusted God and obeyed Him anyway. He found his place called "there."

My hope is that you will read this booklet and become convinced that the Lord is willing to take care of you and He wouldn't ask you to do something for Him in your own strength. God will provide everything you need to be successful (Phil. 4:19). But it does require you to trust Him and be obedient when He calls you to take a step of faith.

Let God Use You

[Elijah] was a man subject to like passions as we are, and he prayed earnestly that it might not rain: and it rained not on the earth by the space of three years and six months.

James 5:17, brackets mine

The Bible gives very little background information on Elijah. It wasn't his pedigree or education that brought him into a position of influence and power. And yet, he was mightily used of God.

Elijah wasn't a perfect person. At one point, he became so despondent that he asked God to kill him (1 Kgs. 19:4). But he still called fire down from heaven three times (1 Kgs. 18:36–38, 2 Kgs. 1:9–13), was the first person to raise someone from the dead (1 Kgs. 17:17–24), caused the greatest revival in history up to that point (1 Kgs. 18:21–40), started and ended a three-year drought (1 Kgs. 17:1, 18:41–45), and multiplied food miraculously (1 Kgs. 17:8–16).

On top of all that, he is one of only two men in the Bible (along with Enoch in Genesis 5:21–24) who never died—he was caught up alive into heaven (2 Kgs. 2:11). There is a lot we can learn from a man like Elijah, both positive and negative.

Elijah was a nobody until he received a word from God. It was the revelation the Lord gave him that put him into a position of leadership. Likewise, anyone who is born again, baptized in the Holy Spirit, and has a relationship with the Lord, has a revelation too.

Just as Elijah's revelation from God put him into a position of influence, anyone who has a revelation of God has the potential to influence others. The only difference is that Elijah knew what he had and was bold enough to speak.

When I was younger, I was an introvert. I couldn't look a person in the face and talk to them. I was fine around friends and family, but talking to strangers petrified me. One time, a man greeted me on the street and said, "Good morning." He was two blocks away and I was sitting in my car before I said, "Good morning," in response! I thought, *There must be something wrong with me!* It was because I was so timid and focused on what people would think of me.

When I first started ministering, I was so nervous and worried about what people would think of me that I would rush through my notes. It seemed like I would finish my whole sermon in five minutes! It was pitiful.

After one of my meetings, someone came up to me and said, "You've got some really good things to share. If you loved the people more than you love yourself, you could be a blessing." What this man said felt like a knife going into me, but he was right. I was only worried about what other people thought about me and not about them.

It takes more than knowing you're called to effectively serve the Lord. You also have to be bold enough to pursue it. And sometimes that means speaking things from the Lord that just aren't popular.

Speak the Word

And Elijah the Tishbite, who was of the inhabitants of Gilead, said unto Ahab, As the LORD God of Israel liveth, before whom I stand, there shall not be dew nor rain these years, but according to my word.

1 Kings 17:1

Many people have been intimidated by the ungodly, and they aren't boldly speaking the truth they have from the Lord. King Ahab "*did evil in the sight of the Lord above all that* were *before him*" (1 Kgs. 16:30), so it was no small feat for Elijah to stand up and speak a word from God to him.

Ahab and his wicked wife Jezebel had outlawed the worship of the true God and instituted Baal worship as the state religion, feeding Baal's prophets at their expense (1 Kgs. 18:19). They were killing anyone who claimed to be a prophet of the Lord God of Israel (1 Kgs. 18:13). Elijah was putting his life at risk to deliver a word from the Lord.

During the COVID pandemic of 2020, the government declared that churches were nonessential and tried to stop people from worshipping together. During the initial phase of this, I decided to voluntarily cooperate, and we scaled back some things just to be good neighbors.

But once I found out that Colorado's governor was trying to restrict things beyond what the state constitution allowed, I drafted a letter cosigned by 700 other ministers informing him that our voluntary cooperation was over. And it caused no small stir! We even received a cease-and-desist letter during one of our events here at Charis. I could have been arrested!

The State of Colorado sued us twice, and we sued them twice. Eventually, the U.S. Supreme Court ruled in favor of some churches in other states that fought against lockdowns. And because of that, Colorado backed down, and we came through it.

We had to take a stand on what the Bible said about these things. We told the authorities that we were not going to forsake the assembling of ourselves together (Heb. 10:25). And because of that, our influence has increased, Charis Bible College is growing, and we have launched the Gospel Truth Network on television and online. But those things wouldn't have happened if we didn't take a stand.

What if Elijah hadn't spoken this prophecy to King Ahab? The drought may have occurred anyway, but Elijah wouldn't have been able to use it to affect the nation. The people would have dismissed the drought as a natural occurrence.

If every pastor and church in our county would have stood with us against the state of Colorado, there may have never been a court battle. But too many Christians want to stay hidden in their prayer closets, waging spiritual battles in private.

Now, I'm not against taking authority over spiritual things in Jesus' name, but you also need to put feet to your prayers. Just as faith without works is dead (James 2:17 and 20), so prayer without works is dead. You need to get out of the prayer closet and start serving the Lord because God works through people.

Elijah was bold enough to speak before there was any proof that what he was saying would come to pass. That took faith and great courage. And when the drought came as promised, Elijah became the most sought-after man in the nation.

People Are Hungry for Truth

As the LORD thy God liveth, there is no nation or kingdom, whither my lord hath not sent to seek thee: and when they said, He is *not* there; *he took an oath of the kingdom and nation, that they found thee not.*

1 Kings 18:10

King Ahab and his wife Jezebel had forbidden worship of the true God, instituting Baal worship (1 Kgs. 16:32). They killed the prophets of the Lord (1 Kgs. 18:4), and Elijah was putting himself in harm's way by declaring God's word to them. But when we speak forth the truths God has shown us, just like Elijah did, the truths we speak will ultimately prevail.

These days, Christianity is being attacked. As a result, too many ministers feel like they need to share biblical truths in a subtle way so that they don't offend anybody. But you aren't going to win people over by compromising and trying to become like them. That won't work, because the Gospel is offensive.

There are so many churches that have moderated their worship service and preaching so that it won't be confrontational. They think this would make an unbeliever more likely to attend their church. Then, once they get inside the doors, they'll be converted.

Since the "seeker sensitive" movement came into prominence, it has produced churches with large attendance numbers, but few who are truly born again. Since these ministers only give their congregations small amounts of the Word, it works like an inoculation (like what people get against measles and other diseases). People are going to church each week, thinking they are in right standing with God because they are going through all the motions, but they aren't being born again because they aren't hearing the true Gospel.

I've heard it said that preaching the true Gospel will cause a revival or a riot, but it won't leave people indifferent. Unfortunately, indifference is where many churches are today. There are churches that shut their doors during Covid and never reopened them. But then there were churches—like those led by pastors Rob McCoy, Che Ahn, Jack Hibbs, and others—that stood strong, resisted government mandates, and kept preaching the Gospel. And because of those things, they grew exponentially.

We took a real risk in standing up for the truth. I could have been arrested and people said we could lose our nonprofit status as a ministry. At some point, my wife Jamie looked at me and said, "I hate this!" I said, "I hate this too, but what choice do we have?" And as it turned out, standing our ground was one of the best decisions we could have made.

You see, people aren't looking for someone who will compromise. King Ahab sent his men looking for Elijah because Elijah's words were true. And that's why these churches and our ministry have grown in influence. People are hungry for the truth and are drawn to people who stand for what is right.

Let People See God in You

If you get a word from God, you've got to speak it, even if it looks like there is no chance of it ever coming to pass. But then, when things begin to happen, people will begin to recognize that it was God speaking through you.

I remember in the days running up to the Y2K "crisis," there were Christians who were saying it would be the beginning of the tribulation period. The secular experts and media were declaring that when clocks turned from 1999 to 2000, computer systems around the world and everything integrated with them—including the power grid—would come to a crashing halt.

I know a minister who was actually selling things in his church like guns, food supplies, and other survival gear. It was a big deal in the body of Christ. Churches and Christians were expecting the worst-case scenario just like the secular world.

About two years before Y2K was supposed to happen, I began to say, "Thus saith the Lord, this is a hoax. It's not going to happen." Most people didn't believe me because so many Christian leaders were proclaiming it was going to be a major deal—it was going to change everything.

I remember being on a radio program in the Dallas-Fort Worth area, and the host was asking me about these things. I said, "I don't believe it's real." And this guy really got on my case! He publicly rebuked me on the radio. He called me a false prophet and just blasted me.

I didn't have any way of proving it at the time, but the Lord had shown me things that led me to believe that Y2K was going to be a non-event. One of those things was that our *Gospel Truth* program was scheduled to launch on television on January 3, 2000. I even recorded a message that said, "If you're seeing me right now, that means Y2K didn't happen." That's just how confident I was in my belief.

So, when Y2K came and went, and nothing happened, it turned out to be the biggest hoax the body of Christ has ever endorsed. And our income just began to go up exponentially. I believe a lot of that increase came because I spoke on it two years in advance and countered those things. Suddenly, people began to respond, and our influence increased.

That's what happened with Elijah. If he had kept to himself what God had shown him, it wouldn't have had any impact. And this is what's happening with a lot of Christians today. They're not speaking against the wokeness and ungodliness that's being promoted in our culture.

They don't agree with it, but they just stay in their closet and pray. They won't speak the truth. And because of that, they won't have any influence for God.

Resist Pressure

Sometimes, the first step of obedience isn't necessarily speaking a word from the Lord to a king. But stepping into God's calling for your life may challenge the relationships you have with the people around you.

Back when the Lord really touched my life on March 23, 1968, one of the first things I did was share my experience with my Baptist church. That next morning, I got up in front of everyone and tried to explain what happened.

I had already turned myself inside out when I was in the presence of the Lord and confessed every sin I committed (or even thought about committing). And instead of killing me on the spot, God overwhelmed me with His unconditional love. So, talking to my church should have been relatively easy.

But when I started sharing about God's love, how I would "never rededicate myself again," and used the phrase "filled with the Holy Spirit," I may as well have cursed.

Those people got offended and the leadership started criticizing me. It was not well received.

One of the next things that happened was I had a strong impression from the Lord to quit college. At the time, the Vietnam War was going on, which meant I would lose my student deferment and be eligible for the draft. I would also lose the monthly payment from my father's Social Security benefits, which I received because he died when I was twelve years old.

Beyond those things, I would be criticized by the people in my church. You see, our church had ties to the local Baptist seminary, so the people there put a strong emphasis on education. And every member of my extended family—with the exception of one uncle who was a farmer—had been schoolteachers. So, coming out and announcing that I was quitting college could cause all kinds of problems.

But, when I got it in my mind that quitting school was what the Lord intended for me, I decided to test these things by announcing my decision to some people who were very influential in my life. One of those people was a schoolteacher who also happened to be a close friend of my mother. She had been very critical of me when I suggested I may leave college. But when I visited her and said I was sure the Lord was calling me out, she responded, "I'd give anything to have what you've got."

After I got over the shock of her confession, she went on to tell me that at her age (probably in her forties or fifties) she still wasn't sure of God's will for her life. And here I was, a teenager, stepping out in faith because I believed I had heard from the Lord. That one decision, possibly more than any other, set my life on a course that has brought me to where I am today.

One Step at a Time

And the word of the LORD came unto him, saying, Get thee hence, and turn thee eastward, and hide thyself by the brook Cherith, that is before Jordan. And it shall be, that thou shalt drink of the brook; and I have commanded the ravens to feed thee there.

1 Kings 17:2–4

Elijah didn't have all the answers or know what would happen next when he spoke the prophecy to King Ahab (1 Kgs. 17:1). But taking that step opened the door to the Lord's provision.

15

God doesn't reveal His complete plan immediately. He reveals His will to us one step at a time. After we take the first step, He shows us the next. Why should the Lord show us step two or beyond if we haven't obeyed step one? That would just make us more accountable. So, don't try to figure out the next step until you have acted on what you know to do now.

The Lord told Elijah to go to the brook Cherith. He had already commanded the ravens to bring Elijah bread and meat "there" every morning and evening. It was miraculous. But notice, the Lord didn't send the provision to where Elijah was at the time. A quarterback doesn't throw the football to where the receiver is but to where the receiver is going. Elijah's miracle wasn't given to him where he was but where the Lord was sending him.

Each of us has a place called "there," where the provision of God is waiting. The Lord never fails to provide, but people often fail to receive because they aren't all "there." If Elijah had not gone to his place called "there," his disobedience would not have stopped God's faithfulness. But he would not have received the provision. It was over "there," by the brook Cherith.

This is exactly what is happening to many of us. The Lord has placed something on our hearts to say or do. But if we haven't obeyed, we aren't in our place called "there." We aren't seeing God's provision, because we aren't in that place of obedience.

I've heard many people say the Lord told them to attend Charis Bible College. But they just can't see how it could happen. They want to see the Lord's provision before they go "there." That's not how it works.

Some of you are not seeing God's provision because you aren't doing what He has told you to do. This doesn't mean the Lord is punishing you. If Elijah hadn't gone "there," he would have lost his provision, but the Lord had already sent the ravens to provide for Elijah "there." The Lord has provision for you too, but it's "there."

Obedience Matters

You can't necessarily see your place called "there" from where you are. You just have to step out in faith and do what God has told you to do. The provision isn't where you are—it's "there." It's found while you're out doing what God has told you to do. Many people are waiting to see the provision before they step out, but God said to Elijah, "I have already commanded the ravens to feed you there!" So, he went (1 Kgs. 17:5).

The brook Cherith must have been at least two or three miles long. How did Elijah know which spot to stop at along the brook? He knew he was in the right place because God had already spoken to the ravens, and they could certainly fly there quicker than he could walk. Therefore, he knew he was in the right place when he saw the provision of bread and flesh.

God had already sent the provision. All Elijah had to do was obey. Obedience matters. Consider what would have happened if Elijah hadn't obeyed. God's provision would have just sat there rotting, and Elijah could have starved.

If I had not followed the Lord's leading to quit college, I may have graduated, gotten a job as a schoolteacher, and had some influence on somebody's life, but you would have never heard of me. Instead, I was drafted into the Army, sent to Vietnam, served as a chaplain's assistant, and spent upwards of fifteen hours a day studying the Word of God.

I may have left for Vietnam as a Baptist, but I didn't come home as one. The Word deposited on the inside of me eventually came alive through the power of the Holy Spirit and, as I went into ministry, I began sharing with others the truths that had changed my life. My provision wasn't at college or even in my Baptist church. The Lord led me to a place where I could receive directly from Him, and it changed my life. But I had to be obedient.

The Lord may not be leading you to a war zone, but there is a place of provision for your life that requires some risk. God is calling you "there." And if you don't put your trust in Him and go, you may miss out on what He has for you.

There is a place for obedience. Obedience doesn't change God's heart toward you, but if you aren't obedient, you can certainly make it hard on yourself. God has a purpose for you. He has placed a call on your life.

Supernatural provision has already been sent to accomplish whatever God has told you to do, but it's "there." Sad to say, many people don't go there because they are doing their own thing, in their own timing, and in their own way. But there is an anointing on being obedient to God and doing what He says.

Access by Faith

Therefore being justified by faith, we have peace with God through our Lord Jesus Christ: by whom also we have access by faith into this grace wherein we stand, and rejoice in hope of the glory of God.

Romans 5:1–2

I preach the grace of God as strong as anybody I know, but I also preach that you've got to be obedient and take action. There are a lot of people who get a partial revelation of grace, and that just leads them into being lazy and sloppy. They think they don't have to do anything at all to receive from God. But I don't believe that.

I know I don't deserve anything based on my own goodness. But I also know that even though God has given everything by grace, I must use faith to access it. God is waiting on us to take steps of faith. So, you need to do what God has told you to do. And if you can't do it all at once, just take one step in that direction. And when you take a step, you'll find out that God will show you the next step and things will begin to start working.

That's what we tell people who believe they're called to go to our Charis Bible College. Even if they can't see everything God has planned for them, they need to take a step in faith. We encourage them to at least fill out an application. That's at least a start. If they do that, I believe they'll start to see God's provision. Then, they'll take another step and continue moving forward.

Right after Jamie and I got married, I felt like it was the beginning of a brand-new chapter in my life. So, I quit my job and went full-time into ministry. (In hindsight, I know that was wrong, and I should have kept working until the ministry really took off, but I just hadn't connected the dots yet.)

I started praying ten to twelve hours a day in tongues, sitting next to the phone, and waiting for somebody to invite me to come minister. That's not very smart, but my heart was right. I was looking to God, and I didn't really know what to do, but I thought that somehow there had to be opportunities for me to minister. And amazingly, after a week or so of doing that, that phone rang!

It was a man I had met two years before at a Bible study and we had just hit it off. We exchanged phone numbers and planned to stay in touch, but that was the only contact I ever had with him up to that point.

Receive Opportunities

Out of the blue, this guy called and asked me to minister to a group of Baptist students on a church retreat. So, I went. There were about forty-five students, and forty of them received the baptism of the Holy Spirit with evidence of speaking in tongues. It was awesome! But when they went back to their Baptist church, the pastor hit the roof, called all the parents, and told them it was of the devil.

All but four or five of those kids ended up walking away and renouncing the experience, but the ones who stayed asked me, "What are we going to do?" And I said, "Well, I'll come over there and start holding Bible studies." And I did that for six months.

These people ended up getting kicked out of their churches, so they said, "This is our church now." I tried to tell them I wasn't a pastor. But they said, "You can call it anything you want to, but this is where we're fed, and we don't have anywhere else to go." So, I became a pastor by default, and I ministered to those people for two years.

After that, I pastored two other churches, led six Bible studies in three states, went on radio, and started traveling.

We just kept going until we reached where we are today. We just kept moving forward, taking one step at a time.

I obeyed God, went where I believed He wanted me to go, and did what I knew to do. And step by step, the Lord started opening doors. And here I am, decades later ministering to a potential audience of more than six billion people around the world on television and discipling people through Charis Bible College.

I saw a picture of these things not long after the Lord touched my life in 1968. I felt like the truths God was showing me in His Word were so powerful that I needed to share them all over the world. And I believed God was going to give me that opportunity, but that's about all I knew. I didn't know how it was going to happen. I didn't have any clue, but it has come to pass.

God is faithful if you will just step out and do whatever you can to move toward what you believe He is calling you to do. I didn't do it perfectly. I should have been working a secular job back when I was ministering to only five people. And because of it, my wife and I went through a lot of hardships that weren't God's will. And yet, God took care of us, and we survived.

Be Encouraged

I have been young, and now *am old; yet have I not seen the righteous forsaken, nor his seed begging bread.*

Psalm 37:25

When we were just getting started in the ministry, I thought that I would be sinning against God if I worked a secular job. Since I was called to the ministry, I believed I had to make one hundred percent of my living from the ministry.

When we were pastoring our first little church in Seagoville, Texas, we were in trouble. We were starving. Jamie was eight months pregnant, and we went for two weeks with no food and nothing but water.

At about that time, we were having a midweek service, and there were only a few people there. To give some perspective, twelve people was a large crowd for our church, and most of the time it was just five people. So, we'd hold our midweek services at people's houses.

That night, we were over at a lady's house, and it was only two weeks before Joshua, our first child, was going to be born. We had to come up with $600 to have our baby at the hospital, and we had just gone two weeks without any food and nothing but water.

Now, some of you can't relate to this because when you say you're broke, you may have $1,000 in the bank and $2,000 worth of bills to pay, but you've still got money. When I say that Jamie and I were broke, I mean that we didn't have anything—zippo, zero, zilch, nada.

The first year that Jamie and I were married, our entire income was $1,253. And that was with $100 a month for rent. I have no idea how we even survived. So, in the natural, we had no hope of getting $600.

Now, I wasn't going to tell anybody that we had a need, and I wasn't going to ask them for help. I didn't want to unintentionally manipulate anyone into giving to us because King David wrote, "I've never seen the righteous forsaken, or their seed begging bread" (Ps. 37:25). But we were struggling, and coming up with that money was heavy on my mind.

I just got up that night and told everyone, "I don't have anything to give you. I need *you* to pray for *me*." And they all just laughed because they didn't realize the gravity of our situation. Here I was, the pastor of this little church, so I should have been able to minister. But I just didn't have anything. So, we just turned on the television to watch the *700 Club*, and Kenneth Copeland was preaching.

Faith Overcomes the World

For whatsoever is born of God overcometh the world: and this is the victory that overcometh the world, even *our faith.*

1 John 5:4

When we sat down to watch Kenneth Copeland on television, he was ministering from 1 John 5:4, which says faith is the victory that overcomes the world. And when he quoted that verse, I thought, *Kenneth, I've preached on that. I know it, and I tried, but it didn't work.* And it was just like he knew what I was thinking. Because the next thing Kenneth said was, "Don't tell me that you tried it. It doesn't say that you try. You just do it!"

If you've ever watched our *Gospel Truth* program, it's not uncommon for me to say something like, "I believe the Lord is speaking to someone right now." But back in the early days of our ministry, when it seemed like Kenneth was responding to my thoughts through the television, it wasn't something I was prepared for!

As you can imagine, I was shocked. So, I responded in my mind, thinking, *But I'm doing all I know to do!* And it was like every thought I had, Kenneth countered it. I really believe that God was speaking supernaturally through him to me. It was the Lord encouraging me and reminding me of what I already knew.

Our faith is the victory that overcomes the world. It didn't say it *might* overcome the world. When we look at our circumstances and it seems like everyone and everything is against us, the enemy tries to use those things to get us to quit and give up before we see our victory. But faith quenches all the fiery darts of the devil (Eph. 6:16). Faith will overcome the world.

You see, I tried, and I didn't think those things were working for me. I was just ready to give up. However, after receiving some encouragement from Kenneth Copeland's teaching, I submitted. I said, "All right, God, I believe!"

It's like when a person gets bucked off a horse, they've got to get back on that horse to show who's in charge. I got back on my faith, and I started saying, "In the name of Jesus, we are overcoming this. We are getting our needs supplied!" And when Joshua was born, that money had come in and the hospital bill was taken care of. Praise the Lord!

During those early years, these things just kept happening time and again. We just seemed to live from miracle to miracle, and the Lord just kept meeting our needs "there." Since then, we've learned some things about prosperity and found out that living in God's blessing is even better than receiving miracles. But those things built our faith and encouraged us to just keep going.

Don't Panic

And the ravens brought him bread and flesh in the morning, and bread and flesh in the evening; and he drank of the brook. And it came to pass after a while, that the brook dried up, because there had been no rain in the land.

1 Kings 17:6–7

Elijah was obeying God in his place called "there" when the brook dried up. And worse yet, he's the one who caused it to happen! Remember, it was Elijah's own prophecy that caused the drought (1 Kgs. 17:1).

It was a serious situation because Elijah needed water to live. A person can only go three days without water before their body shuts down. Seven days without water, and a person could die. You can go forty days without food, but you can't go very long without water. But Elijah didn't move just because the brook dried up.

In a situation like that, when the supply has dried up and something has to change, most people wouldn't wait for a word from God. They would feel like they had to do something, and they would act out of panic. There have been so many times in our own ministry when it looked like the end was near, and I didn't know what to do. I prayed and asked God, but I didn't have a new word.

I didn't have any different instructions than what I was already doing. Everything in the natural was screaming, "You have to do something! You can't just sit there!" But really, until God spoke, I couldn't do anything else. I had already trusted Him up to that point, so what else could I do?

Elijah couldn't just sit there and die of thirst. He had to have water. But Elijah had to cooperate with God to get through this ordeal. If he had left the brook without getting a word from God, he may not have heard about going to Zarephath and meeting the widow there (1 Kgs. 17:9). Then, all of the other things that happened in Elijah's ministry wouldn't have come to pass.

It's likely the brook didn't just dry up all at once. It gradually started having less water in it until it got down to a trickle and finally stopped. Elijah could see this coming. In the same way, we can usually see when a season of our life is coming to an end. But a person's thoughts about the situation tend to make them move before they've received a word from God.

The Word doesn't tell us what Elijah was thinking, but apparently, he was so committed to the fact that the Lord had told him to be there at the brook Cherith that he wasn't going to move until he heard from God again.

Be Ready to Move

A few years ago, God began speaking to me about launching a television network. There were a number of reasons why doing so would make sense. One of those things was that the networks our *Gospel Truth* program was already on had restrictions on what I could say or promote, and that really limited us.

As time went on, I was impressed by the Lord that we should be moving forward with some urgency. When I first presented these things to my staff, the people who were familiar with television said it would take about two years to fully develop original programming and have everything ready to launch. But I told them I believed we should do it sooner—like within six months!

To their credit, our teams went above and beyond to make the Gospel Truth Network a reality within a very short period of time. It has just been awesome the way God has sent such talented people to us who have the right heart for our ministry. But it did create another problem in that more was going to be asked of me.

On average, I recorded twenty-two episodes of our daily *Gospel Truth* program every month. But with the new network, I would be recording sixty-six episodes of multiple programs each month. I would be busier than a one-armed paperhanger! That meant I had to change how I did things.

At some point, after forty-five years in traveling ministry, the Lord got through to my lightning-fast mind that

I was actually in media ministry. So, I announced that we would end the events we were holding around the country and elsewhere. We still host meetings in Woodland Park, and I may occasionally visit churches and join other meetings via livestream, but our ministry will no longer send a dedicated team on the road to hold events.

When we held our last event in Dallas, Texas, it was a celebration of all the things the Lord had done through our traveling ministry all those years. And some people shared things from the platform that were encouraging, but at the same time confirmed that we were moving into something new.

You see, this ministry traditionally reached people through meetings and was supported primarily by a single half-hour, five-days-a-week television program. Now, we could double the size of the ministry and exponentially increase our reach by broadcasting twenty-four hours a day, seven days a week. But again, I had to take a step in faith.

Like Elijah, who left behind the brook and the ravens and went to Zarephath to meet the widow, we were leaving behind our traveling ministry and stepping into something that would offer even greater provision. We found a new place called "there."

Someone Is Waiting

And the word of the LORD came unto him, saying,
Arise, get thee to Zarephath, which belongeth to
Zidon, and dwell there: behold, I have commanded
a widow woman there to sustain thee.

1 Kings 17:8–9

God led Elijah to a new place called "there." And the Lord had already spoken to this widow, just as He had done with the ravens.

This is important because this widow wasn't just anyone. Elijah wasn't just led by circumstances to the first person he ran into. God sent him to a specific woman (Luke 4:26) and had already commanded her to sustain him. Perhaps she had heard about Elijah's prophecy and knew that the drought had been caused by the man of God. Perhaps she believed the Lord would send Elijah her way because she knew she was supposed to sustain him.

It's also possible God showed her that He was going to miraculously provide for her throughout the drought. We don't know the message she received from God, but we know the Lord had already spoken to her heart. He had already commanded her to sustain Elijah.

When Elijah arrived in Zarephath, this widow was out picking up sticks. That doesn't seem like anything special. She wasn't out there praying or doing anything "holy." She was just picking up sticks so she could make a fire and cook her last little bit of food (1 Kgs. 17:12). This may not seem very significant, but she was "there."

For some people, had they been in the situation of this widow, they would have thought, *It's my last little bit of food. It's my last day. I give up!* They would have been back at their house griping and complaining. They might have been depressed or desperately praying for God to do something. But this widow was just "there," doing what she knew to do. This put her in the right place at the right time.

Sometimes we want to do all these super-spiritual things. We want God to do something in a spectacular fashion. Yet, we often encounter the most awesome miracles just by doing the everyday things God has called us to do.

We could receive a word from the Lord while talking to someone at the store, being kind to neighbors, or loving our co-workers. The Word says that "*some have entertained angels unawares*" (Heb. 13:2). Many of us are down at the church building looking for a heavenly vision or an angel to walk through the door when the truth is we pass them on the street.

If we aren't living the Christian life in everyday things, we could be missing out on God's blessing. We could miss out on our miracle because we are too spiritual! If this woman hadn't been there just picking up sticks, which was really an insignificant thing, she could have missed her miracle.

You Have to Be 'There'

But seek ye first the kingdom of God, and his righteousness; and all these things shall be added unto you.

Matthew 6:33

There's a man who's been overseeing the construction of our Charis Bible College student housing in recent years who was sent to us by God. There's just no other way to explain it.

This man had been involved in major building projects for years in the secular world. He helped build professional sports stadiums and arenas in a number of large cities. He was even part of building the Sphere in Las Vegas. A few years ago, we held a partner banquet at one of our events where our CEO Billy Epperhart met this man. As it turned out, he had been a partner with us for a long time.

This man's testimony was that he received a word from the Lord twenty years before. God told him that he would construct buildings "here and there." At the time, this man was working on a project in Jacksonville, Florida. That was the "here" the Lord spoke about.

When this man and his wife first came to Woodland Park to check out our Charis campus, he drove past our main gate and saw the sign that says, "Welcome to your place called 'there.'" This man and his wife took it as confirmation that they were doing the right thing in coming to Colorado to help us. So, they just left everything behind, and he came to work for our ministry.

Here was a man who built things worth billions of dollars that are seen by millions of people in person and on television, and I didn't ask God to send him. The Lord just led him to us. I'm sure he had many other lucrative opportunities, but he followed the leading of the Lord. He was seeking the kingdom first and found his place called "there," trusting that everything else would be taken care of.

God has sent some of the most anointed people on the planet to our ministry. But if I hadn't taken steps of faith and done the things He's told me to do, he wouldn't have sent these people. The Lord would have still been speaking to them, but I wouldn't have been able to receive them.

I would have missed what God was trying to do. That's because I wouldn't have been in a position to accommodate all of the things God wanted them to do here. I had to be in *my* place called "there" first.

Serve Others

So he arose and went to Zarephath. And when he came to the gate of the city, behold, the widow woman was there gathering of sticks: and he called to her, and said, Fetch me, I pray thee, a little water in a vessel, that I may drink.

1 Kings 17:10

If you were like the widow, getting ready to cook your last little bit of food and then die, and somebody came to you and asked for a drink of water, would you give it to him? How about if both you and your refrigerator were full and everything looked good for you and a stranger came up to you and asked for a drink of water, would you give it to him?

For this woman to serve Elijah first says a lot about her. I believe that's one of the reasons why God chose her over everyone else to provide for His messenger. She was a giver. She was someone who didn't just think only of herself. Here she was on what seemed to be her last day on the face of the earth, yet she was willing to serve somebody. Many of us aren't willing to serve anybody on a good day, much less a bad one.

Remember, Elijah knew this was "the" woman. He didn't ask her for assistance randomly to check her out. He called out to her on purpose. But when Elijah called for a piece of bread (1 Kgs. 17:11), she told him, "I just have a handful of meal and a little oil." Then she went on to say, "*I am gathering two sticks, that I may go in and dress it for me and my son, that we may eat it, and die*" (1 Kgs. 17:12).

Now that doesn't seem like a very positive confession. On the surface, it appears as if the woman is in total unbelief. Yet the Word reveals that God had commanded this widow to feed Elijah (1 Kgs. 17:9). This was a divine connection, and she already had a word from God.

I believe the widow was saying these things as a way of asking Elijah, "Are you the one who was sent by God?" God had spoken to her, and she had a revelation. She believed God would provide for her supernaturally.

That widow probably had been going through this same routine every day, and now, when it looked like she was down to her last little bit of meal and oil, here comes this man asking for something to eat in a time of drought and famine. That's when he demanded, "*Make me thereof a little cake first, and bring it unto me, and after make for thee and for thy son*" (1 Kgs. 17:13).

Offer a Chance to Give

For thus saith the Lord God of Israel, The barrel of meal shall not waste, neither shall the cruse of oil fail, until the day that the Lord sendeth rain upon the earth.

1 Kings 17:14

Elijah gave the widow the word of God—the same word that he had been living under that had been meeting his needs. We shouldn't just ask people for money without giving them something to stand on. We shouldn't encourage people to give without giving them the Word of God to anchor their faith.

People shouldn't be giving to you because of your charisma or need. They should be giving because they've been given God's Word and have been challenged to step out in faith. Elijah challenged this woman's faith and gave her the word of the Lord to stand on, *"And she went and did"* (1 Kgs. 17:15). She obeyed the word of God.

Elijah was the prophet of God. He was blessed. Elijah could have eaten at the best restaurant and stayed in the best hotel in Zarephath. He didn't need this widow's food for himself. This was actually a provision for her. By asking her to give the last food she had, Elijah wasn't taking from this woman. He was giving to her. She was sowing a seed that would come back to her and sustain her and her son for years to come. He had to be bold, not just for his sake, but to also confirm and build the faith of the widow who was giving to him.

Ministers need to do the same thing when they receive offerings and encourage people to give. One of the ways Satan has hindered the flow of finances in the body of

Christ is through preachers who view the request for tithes and offerings as a plea for finances for themselves.

If they see it that way, they're always going to be bashful and apologetic when they call God's people to bring their tithes and offerings. They're going to be timid because they don't want to portray themselves as trying to take from the people. But the truth is, we're asking the people to give for their own sake, not for ours!

It's an irreversible law of God that we have to give to receive (Luke 6:38). If we really understood and believed this, we as ministers would be as bold as Elijah to encourage people to give. We aren't taking money from people; we are giving them an opportunity to invest, with dividends that are out of this world.

Elijah said, "Give to me first," but this wasn't just a one-time deal. The widow did this every day until the drought ended. The Bible doesn't tell us the exact length of time the drought persisted while she was providing for Elijah, but it was probably around two and a half to three years that this little bit of oil and meal sustained them (1 Kgs. 17:15–16). She didn't give to Elijah one time and then receive three years' supply of oil and meal. There was always that tiny little bit, but it never failed!

Giving and Receiving

Being in the right place and connected to the right people doesn't just benefit you. It also benefits the people God uses to meet your needs. Giving will bless the giver just as much as it blesses the person receiving the gift.

One time, I was ministering at Pastor Greg Mohr's church in Decatur, Texas, and there was a woman who came up to me after the meeting. The previous year, I had ministered to her, and she had been delivered from some things. She had been committed to a mental health facility as a patient, and the Lord delivered her from her condition. It was awesome!

But when she came to this meeting, the woman said she was believing for more. Even though she was released from the facility as a patient, she still worked as a custodian and lived there. She was asking me to pray with her for a new place to live and a new job.

It was a situation like Elijah and the widow. She knew that giving would open doors to her provision, but she didn't think she had much to give since her job didn't pay her that much. All she had was a little change purse with her, and it had about $83 of cash and coins in it. That was everything she had until the next payday. That's when I said, "Give me all of it!"

Now, you can imagine what people would probably say if they saw me doing that. So, when she emptied her change purse and gave me all her money, I turned around and gave it to her pastor, Greg Mohr. Then we agreed with this woman in prayer.

The very next day, someone who wasn't from that church gave her a car. It wasn't a new car, but it was new to her. This person didn't know the woman's situation, but they just felt led by the Lord to give it to her. What a blessing!

Next, her mother called her out of the blue. They hadn't spoken in a very long time. The mother had cut her off when she went into the mental facility. The mother felt bad that she hadn't kept in touch and offered to let the daughter move back home. So, she not only got another place to live, but got her relationship with her mother restored. By the end of that week, she had a job that paid her twice as much money as she was making before.

But what would have happened if I looked at what that woman had to offer and said, "Aw, you just keep it. I know you need that money for other things." No! I saw it as an opportunity to get her out of the situation she was in and lead her into more provision.

Giving Affects Others

And the Lord heard the voice of Elijah; and the soul of the child came into him again, and he revived.

1 Kings 17:22

This widow's giving not only affected her, but it also affected her son (1 Kings 17:17–24). At some point, the woman's son died. By this time, she had been walking by faith and giving to the man of God first every day for quite some time. Since she had been giving, she could expect to receive. She had a right to make a demand on him to raise up her son.

This is the first instance in Scripture of anyone being raised from the dead. It hadn't been done prior to this time. There was no precedent for it. Seeing someone raised from the dead today is still unusual, but it's not unheard of.

I saw a man raised from the dead while I was ministering in Pritchett, Colorado. My son and wife have been raised from the dead. And I've heard of dozens of people raised from the dead through this ministry and the people who have graduated from Charis.

As a matter of fact, back in the early days of this ministry, when I was believing to see someone raised from the dead, I used to meditate on this passage of Scripture and picture myself as Elijah, raising this boy. But Elijah was the first. He didn't have anybody else's testimony to stand on. He just had to believe God.

The boy's mother was reaching out in faith and making a demand on the power of God that resided in Elijah. All of this started with her believing God's promise about the multiplication of her food. It just goes to show that if we can't believe for that which is least, we can't believe for that which is greater (Luke 16:10–13).

Back when we received a phone call in the early morning hours of March 4, 2001, that our youngest son Jonathan Peter was dead, we felt all the natural emotions a parent would feel. But as we began the long drive from where we lived in the mountains to the hospital in Colorado Springs, we just began thanking God for all the good things He had done for us over the years.

By that time in our lives, my wife and I had been walking with the Lord for decades. God had always blessed us and taken care of us through the years as we trusted Him. So, I told Jamie we were about to see the greatest miracle of our lives, and we just kept rejoicing all the way to the hospital.

When we got to the hospital, our oldest son Joshua met us at the door and said, "I don't know what happened, but about ten minutes after I called you, Jonathan Peter sat up in the morgue and started talking." Praise the Lord, God met us "there" and raised our son from the dead!

God Directs Our Steps

Thy word is *a lamp unto my feet, and a light unto my path.*

Psalm 119:105

God directs our steps, but He doesn't show us the end of the path from the beginning. He gives us just enough light to know where to go next.

He only shows us one step at a time because He loves us. I have people come to me all the time who know that

God wants them to attend Charis Bible College, but they hesitate because they can't see how everything is going to work out. They just don't see how they are going to get "there."

They are trying to see the end from the beginning. I remember one man coming into my office who said he was certain that God had told him to go to Charis, but then he started telling me all the reasons he thought it wouldn't work out.

He told me about his job, his girlfriend, and the opinions of his parents and pastor. When he was finished, he said, "So, what do you think?" I said, "You lost me the moment you said God told you to do it. If God told you to do it, then forget all the rest."

It's really pretty simple—if the Lord tells you to do something, do it! When God Almighty, Who has a universe to run, takes the time to talk to you and tell you to do something, why would you reason it all out? Why would you try to decide whether you're going to do it or not? Something is seriously wrong with that approach.

If that's the way you think, you aren't absolutely convinced that God is working for your best interest. God's plans for you are better than your plans for yourself. When the Lord tells you to do something, just do it!

When we started Charis, I didn't have anybody to help me, and I didn't know what I was doing. But God knew who would go to school there, so it was important that we got started. We had to move forward and start developing God's vision for a Bible college in steps and stages.

I would rather step out in faith doing what I think God is telling me to do and be wrong than not do what He is telling me to because I want to play it safe. God knows what He is doing and the challenges we will face. I don't want any of the miracles that God has put on the inside of me still there when I leave this world. I want to get them all out. I want to be "there" when God needs me to be!

Conclusion

If Elijah hadn't gone to his place called "there," he wouldn't have been in position to receive from God. Many times, people make excuses about why they can't follow the Lord, even though they'll find that He will provide everything they need when they get "there."

I hope that this booklet has encouraged you to pursue whatever God has called you to do. Whether it's enrolling at school, going into ministry, starting a business, or something else the Lord has for you, He has already made the provision for it.

As long as you are obedient to God and just take one step at a time, you will continue being in your place called "there" and you will walk in everything the Lord has for you. I believe you will discover God's very best for your life, and you will be blessed!

FURTHER STUDY

If you enjoyed this booklet and would like to learn more about some of the things I've shared, I suggest my teachings:

- *The Power of Imagination*
- *Don't Limit God*
- *You've Already Got It!*
- *How to Find, Follow, and Fulfill God's Will*
- *10 Reasons It's Better to Have the Holy Spirit*

These teachings are available for free at **awmi.net**, or they can be purchased at **awmi.net/store**.

Go deeper in your relationship with God by browsing all of Andrew's free teachings.

Receive Jesus as Your Savior

Choosing to receive Jesus Christ as your Lord and Savior is the most important decision you'll ever make!

God's Word promises, *"That if thou shalt confess with thy mouth the Lord Jesus, and shalt believe in thine heart that God hath raised him from the dead, thou shalt be saved. For with the heart man believeth unto righteousness; and with the mouth confession is made unto salvation"* (Rom. 10:9–10). *"For whosoever shall call upon the name of the Lord shall be saved"* (Rom. 10:13). By His grace, God has already done everything to provide salvation. Your part is simply to believe and receive.

Pray out loud: "Jesus, I acknowledge that I've sinned and need to receive what you did for the forgiveness of my sins. I confess that You are my Lord and Savior. I believe in my heart that God raised You from the dead. By faith in Your Word, I receive salvation now. Thank You for saving me."

The very moment you commit your life to Jesus Christ, the truth of His Word instantly comes to pass in your spirit. Now that you're born again, there's a brand-new you!

Please contact us and let us know that you've prayed to receive Jesus as your Savior. We'd like to send you some free materials to help you on your new journey. Call our Helpline: **719-635-1111** (available 24 hours a day, seven days a week) to speak to a staff member who is here to help you understand and grow in your new relationship with the Lord.

Welcome to your new life!

Receive the Holy Spirit

As His child, your loving heavenly Father wants to give you the supernatural power you need to live a new life. *"For every one that asketh receiveth; and he that seeketh findeth; and to him that knocketh it shall be opened...how much more shall your heavenly Father give the Holy Spirit to them that ask him?"* (Luke 11:10–13).

All you have to do is ask, believe, and receive! Pray this: "Father, I recognize my need for Your power to live a new life. Please fill me with Your Holy Spirit. By faith, I receive it right now. Thank You for baptizing me. Holy Spirit, You are welcome in my life."

Some syllables from a language you don't recognize will rise up from your heart to your mouth (1 Cor. 14:14). As you speak them out loud by faith, you're releasing God's power from within and building yourself up in the spirit (1 Cor. 14:4). You can do this whenever and wherever you like.

It doesn't really matter whether you felt anything or not when you prayed to receive the Lord and His Spirit. If you believed in your heart that you received, then God's

Word promises you did. *"Therefore I say unto you, What things soever ye desire, when ye pray, believe that ye receive them, and ye shall have them"* (Mark 11:24). God always honors His Word—believe it!

We would like to rejoice with you, pray with you, and answer any questions to help you understand more fully what has taken place in your life!

Please contact us to let us know that you've prayed to be filled with the Holy Spirit and to request the book *The New You & the Holy Spirit*. This book will explain in more detail about the benefits of being filled with the Holy Spirit and speaking in tongues. Call our Helpline: **719-635-1111** (available 24 hours a day, seven days a week).

Call for Prayer

If you need prayer for any reason, you can call our Helpline, 24 hours a day, seven days a week at **719-635-1111**. A trained prayer minister will answer your call and pray with you.

Every day, we receive testimonies of healings and other miracles from our Helpline, and we are ministering God's nearly-too-good-to-be-true message of the Gospel to more people than ever. So, I encourage you to call today!

About the Author

Andrew Wommack's life was forever changed the moment he encountered the supernatural love of God on March 23, 1968: As a renowned Bible teacher and author, Andrew has made it his mission to change the way the world sees God.

Andrew's vision is to go as far and deep with the Gospel as possible. His message goes far through the *Gospel Truth* television program, which is available to over half the world's population. The message goes deep through discipleship at Charis Bible College, headquartered in Woodland Park, Colorado. Founded in 1994, Charis has campuses across the United States and around the globe.

Andrew also has an extensive library of teaching materials in print, audio, and video. More than 200,000 hours of free teachings can be accessed at **awmi.net**.

Contact Information

Andrew Wommack Ministries, Inc.

PO Box 3333
Colorado Springs, CO 80934-3333
info@awmi.net
awmi.net

Helpline: 719-635-1111 (available 24/7)

Charis Bible College

info@charisbiblecollege.org
844-360-9577
CharisBibleCollege.org

Gospel Truth Network

gtntv.com

For a complete list of all of our offices,
visit **awmi.net/contact-us**.

Connect with us on social media.

Sign up to watch anytime, anywhere, for free.

GOSPEL TRUTH
N E T W O R K